# Insurance Claim Steps

## For Roofers and Contractors

# D Cummins

Thompson Legacy Publishing Inc

Insurance Claim Steps

# contents

# CHAPTER 1

# DEDICATION

To my father, you were the best of the best, and your character, kindness, and highly skilled work will never be forgotten.  You are my dad, and I carry your last name and will always remember you in awe.

To my wife who, over the decades, supported me, visited and encouraged me to build an awe-inspiring career, and after months of exhausting hot days on the roofs, you always listened to my boring conversations and still managed to encourage me to get through the work, the owners and sub-contractors, to produce high-quality projects with happy owners. You have always been there for me, from my residential to my commercial career, and for every outrageous and trying year after that!  You are Amazing in every way!

"It Always Will Be" - a song by Willie Nelson.

*3 Story School Mod Bit Roof System*

# Chapter Two

# INTRODUCTION

## How Do You Eat an Elephant

My career asan inspector spanned over 24 years. The total summary of project/job completions was over 9 million+. I only did this job for 12 years. I did not know what a 3-tab shingle was during my first week at a roofing company—that's how new I was to the industry. The only reason they hired me was that I had an Adjusters license. Ultimately I worked for eight high-quality 20-40+ year-long established companies, sometimes overlapping.

**YOU can do this if you read, learn how to inspect weather damage, and learn how to prove it!** Watch YouTube videos about weather damage and how to inspect it. I could not have had a wealthier career without training and working with the best guidance. You can work towards your licensing in your field. If you care about your reputation,always work for a long-standing, A+, high-quality company. They will always want the restorations installed correctly so that you will learn correctly from these companies.

**How Do You Eat an Elephant?**

**One Bite at a Time.**

**-Desmond Tutu and Creighton Abrams**

*Metal Guage*

# Chapter Three

# THank you!

**Thank you for purchasing this** book! If you did so, you are in the construction or restoration business, and an insurance claim (linear) steps must be involved. There are a total of 31 Steps within this book. Some of these steps are general, and some will have detailed notes from me underneath the step. Some will not apply to you. If this is the case, you are probably correct. Every job has details others may not understand. I have worked in this field for over 42 years and 12 years inspecting and general contracting. I completed 40-60+ jobs each year, so reading this book will enlighten you.

# Chapter Four

# THE AUTHOR'S CREDENTIALS

## It Was Hard But a Blast!

My wonderful Father was the most excellent independent contractor on Earth. He started training me to be a painter (free help). I then worked as a painter and worked my way up the work possibilities in construction.  Ultimately, becoming a warranty manager for a production home builder carrying 1-5 subdivisions simultaneously. After I realized your pay is capped when working for a production home builder, no matter your skills or how long you work each week. My career shifted to the inspection side of the building industry.  I wanted to help homeowners (vs .—contractors who sometimes take advantage of them).  So, I became a FEMA Inspector (it's free, by the way).  Then, I became an Insurance Adjuster, and then, as years passed, a licensed Residential and Commercial Roof Inspector and a sub-contractor/general contractor for many named hail storms, windstorms, and hurricanes.   Per the rules, I could not work simultaneously for an insurance or restoration company for the same storm storm/work. In Summary, my credentials include past construction experience (my father was a builder), remodeling houses, and I helped build several homes. Then I went on to inspect "storm damage."  I applied for inspector positions with FEMA and then worked two hurricanes. Then, I applied and tested for an Adjusters' license.

To benefit the property owners directly, I decided to work on the contractor side, so I obtained my residential and commercial roof inspector licenses from https://haagglobal.com/. Many sub-category certificates and awards offered by Haag promoted my experience and accomplishments. They teach you what to look for and how to inspect, photograph, mark the damages, and estimate the costs. You cannot inform a homeowner of weather damage if you don't know the basics of finding, marking, and getting the damages paid for by the homeowner and/or the insurance companies.

These licenses saved me so much time in pre-production, post-production, and while in the field. Get them if you're a serious storm contractor. It seems every company usually has several management and field inspectors obtaining them. And as you know, if you're in this type of business, you typically get Net 5-10% of the job or 20-50% of the net claim after the expenses are paid so that you can imagine your paycheck at the end of each job. It's hard work. But it is well worth the accolades from your homeowners and pay from your company.

Your hats? Accountant, contractor, inspector, production orders, reviewer, sub-contractor management, customer service, GC. Since I was a seasoned storm/field adjuster, roof inspector, and general contractor, my net rate was always 50% of the net claim after expenses were paid. I was obliged to this rate because I was organized and had a well-documented history of completed projects. On the homeowner side, many owners and business owners always referred me to their co-workers, friends, realtors, HOA managers, and Developers.

Another advantage of being organized and detailed in this job is that if you work for the best contracting companies in the storm area with a well-documented track record, the best companies in the industry will call and accept you—usually call and hire you. This means you typically have a lot of job offers from different companies for the same storm or hurricane. It's not a bad problem to have.

Now, you can choose who you want to work for and, more importantly, select your rate! Usually, if assigned immediately to the storm location, you can set up and get your hotel room quickly before they run out.

Be impeccable with your word, education, and training. This is an essential rule to know in this industry. These companies usually work together on the same storm events year by year. They know each other's companies and some of the individuals as well. Be careful what you say!

*Storm Brewing*

Chapter Five

# STOrm Damages Every State, Every Year

As you know, storms, tornadoes, and hurricanes cause damages into the billions. Areas like these need contractors to rebuild and restore each property so families and businesses can return to their "normal" daily lives. As I started inspecting insurance claims/storm damage for each company, I noticed the company had its rules, requests, and mandates with aids to help you succeed in the field, but you are required to wear many hats. The information in this book will be helpful to both sides.  At the beginning of my general contracting career, I noticed storm claims; no matter what state or storm, I always followed the same lineal stages regarding the insurance claim *process*. There might be some changes here and there, but 98% of the homeowner claim processes were the same. The steps within this book can be reviewed and used by *any* insurance adjuster and/or restoration contractor.

# Chapter Six

# TIME MANAGEMENT SOLUTION

I've always been a detailed organizer. So, having these steps in an Excel spreadsheet for every project/owner makes it highly convenient to have everything laid out and ready to go on one or two sheets of paper that you can update in your vehicle or at home each night/morning. All contractors know how many sub-contractors, steps, costs, and how much personnel they'll need to complete a job. However, an insurance claim requires *additional* steps. **<u>Each step</u> within this book may not apply to you,** but the extra steps may be necessary. Maybe you can adjust the order, but it's usually linear. When in doubt, ask your management, and then after approval, inform the insurance adjuster <u>if</u> necessary. Ask your contractor(S)or insurance adjuster if you are on the right path.  If a step is not needed, then skip or delete. All you have to do is mark thru or delete the step(s) you do not like and move forward. The steps may have a comment from me below each text to give you the contractor/inspector. Each step has information, but you can always disregard whatever you feel is unnecessary for your career or job. Every storm or hurricane I worked with, the roofing/contracting companies eventually allowed me to have multiple leads/projects simultaneously. This was because I was organized, and I knew what the "other sides' wants or expectations were and their omittances. Ultimately, your job is to get the adjuster the proof so you can get the supplements approved as soon as possible.

I eventually created spreadsheets during each storm and built upon them during and after each storm. These steps within my spreadsheet will help you minimize your hours and work if you are organized and also keep yourself from making bad mistakes such (*EXAMPLE:*) not remembering you're supposed to meet an owner with his adjuster to review and approve their storm damages.

Remember, to be successful, you must work for a contracting company and have many jobs simultaneously—for various reasons. As they say in the industry, "You Gotta Build Your Pipeline!"

You want to obtain as many jobs/contracts/projects as possible and manage them all simultaneously. Once you review this book, you can start including most of these in your career. Of course, include your own steps/work in this list of steps. Start to build your spreadsheet and include the applicable steps herein.

Due to the organization of a spreadsheet such as this one, I could not carry 40-60 jobs simultaneously, totaling over 1 million in sales each year for 12 years.

My largest <u>net</u> one-job commission was $135k. It was a school with 2" hailstone damage.  The insurance company initially stated they had $500+k and gave them a check.  My partner and I inspected and photographed, and we estimated we had over $2.5 million in damages over the same seven buildings.  Mind you, we were using the same pricing software the insurance companies were using called Xactimate. Later we found out the resistance was due that the insurance adjuster could not write an estimate over"*his* cap" imposed at the time by the insurance company.

Without our expertise, they would have accepted the $500K check and settled, not knowing all buildings had significant damages. The school already had multiple extensive leaks.  Conclusion? The insurance company ended up paying $2 million, and all seven buildings had brand new roofs, complete property hail repairs, and paint.  The first insurance report was paying for one building to be reroofed with leak repairs on two other buildings.  I felt so happy for the kids, teachers, and staff who would then safely live their lives in all buildings once again, and the insurance company was doing what they said they would do in their t.v. commercials!

The best part of my job? Getting the insurance company to pay what the owner deserves and to work for a contractor that repairs and restores the structures back to their current value before the storm event. On top of those parts, I would have to say other bonuses: Standing at the highest point of a roof and looking across the city landscape with a cool breeze on my face every day. I didn't look down. I'm scared of heights.

*Baseball Size Hailstone*

*Softball Size Hailstone*

# Chapter Seven

# Information You May Not Know

## Large Storms Do Have Silver Linings

Storms are a good event for a suburb, town, or city after the storm leaves because your insurance company is legally obligated to restore your home or structure to its original condition <u>and</u> value like before the storm. The storms bring in many skilled people (and some crooks!) to the area to correct the damages caused by the storm event. This means more income for the city or town laborers, restaurants, gas stations, local contracting businesses, and their economy.

Your job is to assess your owner's damages, give him a current value/numbers, get insurance approval, and then repair and restore to better and newer condition than before the storm.

Some insurance adjusters, or some insurance companies, want to ignore the obvious and only release partial monies with lower values and hope the owner goes away, never to ask for the other 60-? % value, which may still be in the insurance company's bank. You need to know your properties and insurance claim steps enough to converse with the insurance adjuster and explain why your owners need more funds (your company can help if you don't know how to estimate or bid). Your owners do not see the construction practices, current pricing and labor prices, and building codes much less requirements and procedures.  Tip:  A Bid means the price you are stating is FINAL".  An Estimate means it's your best price at the time of creation, but not final.  Why It can be adjusted depending on materials and labor price changes, job demands, weather, and unknown possibilities. Unknown code issues, unknown prior damages.  Ultimately, you may need to educate your homeowner to protect them in a way that is proper, correct, and true.   These jobs can take two weeks, but sometimes it can take up to 6 months (depending on the weather and many other issues). These steps will help you learn from start to completion, from A to Z, saving you a lot of time! Remember you want to obtain as many jobs/contracts/projects as possible and manage them all simultaneously. Remember, you do not fix damages; your contractors and sub-contractors will do the restoration. One of many "hats" you will wear will be Project Manager.

Due to this industry, I earned Contractor of the Year for 8 years, among many other awards and certificates. Of course, these steps and spreadsheet usage will pay you an excellent salary if you are organized and adaptable. The money and steps will make you enjoy and cherish your spreadsheet. $3-5-10K a month was not abnormal. **You are paid for the different hats you wear and the size of your projects.**

# BOOK BeneFITS!

This information will save you many hours for your clients and jobs in the field!

We all need more jobs and more time in this business! When you are organized, your pay and tier rise. It raises the bar of your reputation – it sets you apart from the *Sales* guys. It raises the need for your bosses to keep you because they won't have to micro-manage you and lose money.

By following and inserting your steps, these together can create a positive reputation for yourself as a dependable and the reputation of whom to call when leads pop up as long as you prefer to be organized and follow the claim steps.  Being a "benefit" to the storm restoration process will always benefit you and your company. Be HON-EST, honorable, safe, detailed, kind but firm, and follow your State and OSHA rules, and you'll

wake up maybe like me - already retired. You will be streamlining each of your jobs. **Happy owners will refer you.**

# Chapter Nine

# Testimonials

During my career, I was asked to train and manage other individuals on how to work storm claims. First, I would give them this worksheet explaining the steps needed from start to finish. It was explained that when working a storm claim, the insurance process was the same except for a few minor differences depending on the job, the materials, and the contractor's availability. Ultimately, the order depends on the owner, the insurance company, the boss, and you.

I worked for a company in Florida, and I met a person probably under the age of 70; he had a huge three-ring binder that had all of his jobs in sections, and after being there for a couple of months, this binder was huge. Because he didn't fully understand the insurance process, he was overwhelmed; he had heard about me and asked if I wouldn't mind helping him; of course, I gave him the info, and he increased their preproduction, job management, and the pay scale soared. I'm talking about the same year. I was very happy for him, and he did GREAT because he had what it took to apply, work, and complete all his jobs with the insurance company. Now, I think he has his own restoration company. He had what it took to do this claim work.  You show up every day, and you get the job done.  One bite at a time.

On one of my inspection jobs, my owner asked if I could get her son a job with our company doing the same thing. I told her it all depended on his experience, construction knowledge, and whether he could climb a roof. I met her very buff and muscular son; he was intelligent and open to change. From that point forward, he reviewed our job inspections with us and met with our sub-contractors. I let him look at my spreadsheet (Sample in the last chapter of this book, with my notes in italics), and he understood, applied, thrived, and eventually went to work for himself. **If you're not adaptable & organized, then this career is not for you.**

# Chapter Ten

# IT'S TIME TO TAKE A LOOK

## Licenses are not necessary

This job is teachable without you obtaining licenses. Sometimes, if you work for a great local company, they will teach you. If you want to soar and get to know your opponent, get the licenses and as much information as possible. They will increase your commissions exponentially!

BTW, FEMA training is free through their application with the approved contractors. They train you for free and give you their laptops so you can send them the photos and details. When I worked for FEMA, the rate was $25 per property claim, and anyone could inspect about 5-8 houses per day. What do you need to be? <u>Organized</u> and ready to go! I'm sure the rate is a lot higher by now.  This schedule/steps spreadsheet will teach you what storm claims/jobs include and what you may need to do in general.

<u>Feel free to disregard any steps you do not feel apply to your jobs and add any you NEED to remember so it will be out of your head and now on a spreadsheet</u>. Be sure to insert your additional steps in the correct slot/place depending on your company/sub-contractor, claim, or homeowners claim stage. Make sure your spreadsheet is relevant and applicable to you and your projects. Some topics regarding your work, project, or new build may be out of order. Remember, every residential and commercial claim in your state will be handled similarly 98% of the time. The slight differences are acceptable if they are addressed. The steps and notations below will give you a starting point for your jobs and self-care.

The *"Author's notes" are my detailed explanations of each* step notated. Reviewing the steps below may improve your new spreadsheet. Remember, this is *your* time management at stake.

# Chapter Eleven

# Steep Goat Ladder System

You don't have to say no to the homeowner or adjuster. Use this invaluable tool to get the big jobs!

https://thegoatsteepassist.com/

*Steep Goat Ladder System*

# MORE PHOTOS

*Missing Vent /Hole at Center of Main Ridge with In-sulated Metal Roof Panels System*

*Stucco Hail Damage Repairs (Patch, texture, Paint*

*Austin Killeen Hail Storm 2016*

# Chapter Thirteen

# Review Please?

***I hope you are kind enough*** *to give a retired, fellow independent contractor* a 5-star positive review on Amazon. Your review will be read and greatly appreciated! Only purchasers of this book can leave me a review, so it goes a long way, and frankly, they are tough to get with everything moving so fast these days. The easiest way to do this is to aim your smartphone camera at the QR Code below, and when your screen notifies you of a website, tap on the yellow website alert - with your finger, and you'll be taken there so easily....

*QR CODE FOR EASY ACCESS TO LEAVE REVIEW : )*

C

# GENERAL LINEAR CLAIM contractor steps

**Blank Page For Your Use**

# Chapter Fifteen

# Steps 1-13

# STEPS 14-20

14. DURING THE OWNER SIGNATURE MEETING, DON'T FORGET TO GET THEIR FIRST INSURANCE PAYMENT BEFORE YOU LEAVE SO YOU CAN GET TO YOUR MANAGEMENT TO START PROCESSING YOUR JOB!

15. SEND ALL PAPERWORK TO THE OFFICE, WHICH INCLUDES YOUR SIGNED CONTRACT, THE FIRST APPROVED ESTIMATE, THE INSURANCE COMPANY, AND YOUR WORK ORDERS. YOUR JOB IS NOW "IN PROCESS":

*Author's notes:* Your office will explain how they want you to do this and more.

## 16. UPLOAD CONTRACT DOCUMENTS TO YOUR COMPANY:

*Author's notes:* Your insurance adjuster may ask you for the signed contract *before* the estimate from your company has been approved by the insurance company. Remember, what you sent to the insurance company is an estimate, <u>not a bid</u>. There is a difference. Remember an estimate is between you, the homeowner and the insurance company, and it is fluid and can raise or lower project pricing, and the signed contract is between your company and the owner <u>only</u>. A BID means you cannot add *any additional* price increases, unforeseen expenses, or additions to the claim. A BID is a job price at which you are willing to complete the job. It's non-negotiable after the job starts, and it may not be a good place to be unless you're lucky!

## 17. CREATE WORK ORDERS AND UPDATE THE NEXT STEPS: DO NOT START WITHOUT THE INSURANCE COMPANY APPROVING YOUR NUMBERS

*Author's notes:* It's time for the production side of your job to fulfill all of your promises to your owner. Each storm-damaged item needs work orders for your company to schedule and start the repairs. Orders include product selections, sub-contractors, labor,etc. You do not do this until the insurance company approves the your estimates and/or the supplements. You can begin to prepare them, but do not complete and submit them, please, for your own sake. Damaged items do not include "Personal Property," such as a couch, exterior pool lounge chair, clothes, clothes, hallway runner/carpets(non-construction items), etc.

## 18. SEND YOUR SUPPLEMENT ESTIMATE TO YOUR ASSIGNED INSURANCE ADJUSTER FOR APPROVAL:

*Author's notes:*  A Supplement Estimate includes all the damages YOU found that were not on the insurance company's first report. This consists of the items and other items needed to install the system, including accessories and labor correctly. You can list all items on the insurance company's report in one section. However, these same items should now be at current pricing, with accurate descriptions you need to cover the costs, labor & management fees. Then, add the damages the adjuster did not include in his report. Your company should approve the new estimate, and then you send it to the insurance adjuster. Supplement estimates include the damages the insurance company did not list in their first report.  Also, in your supplement estimate, you must include photos of weather damage. This can address the damages you and the owner saw in your pictures of additional damages for the owner.

## 19. HAS INSURANCE COMPANY RECEIVED ANY SUPPLEMENT ESTIMATES FROM YOU?

*Author's notes:* Speak with your management for clarity; they can explain how they want this created, tweaked, and sent to the insurance adjuster. Call the insurance adjuster for approval and ask when the supplement check will be sent to your homeowner so you can tell the homeowner. Kindly get your jobs approved and rolling to production and completion.

## 20. INFORM YOUR OWNER OF THE DATES OF EACH REPAIR OR SYSTEM INSTALLATION AND ASK THEM TO PREPARE THEIR PROPERTY:

*Author's notes:*  Your office will explain how they want you to do all of this, BUT CONFIRM TO YOUR OWNER THAT YOU WILL BE THERE OVERSEEING EACH REPAIR OR RESTORATION.

# Chapter Seventeen

# STEPS 21-31+

21. CALL INSURANCE COMPANY - WHEN ARE THEY MAILING THE ADDITIONAL SUPPLEMENT FUNDS TO YOUR COMPANY OR THE OWNER?

22. THE INSURANCE COMPANY WILL WANT A FINAL INVOICE STATING WHAT ITEMS HAVE BEEN COMPLETED. THIS INCLUDES THE FIRST INSURANCE TOTAL (MINUS ITEMS YOU DID NOT REPAIR AND PERSONAL ITEMS TOTAL). YOUR OWNER HAS TO PAY THEIR DEDUCTIBLE OBLIGATION TO YOU AS WELL.

23. IF ALL SUB-CONTRACTOR BILLS HAVE BEEN PAID AND ALL MONIES HAVE BEEN RECEIVED, THEN SUBMIT TO THE OFFICE FOR YOUR CAP-OUT TO BE PAID!

24. THE INSURANCE COMPANY RELEASES THE FINAL SUPPLEMENTAND/OR DEPRECIATION REIMBURSEMENT (SINCE YOU REPAIRED AND COMPLETED EVERYTHINGIN YOUR HOMEOWNER JOB CONTRACT).  CALLYOUR OWNER & P/U FINAL FUNDS FOR THE OFFICE. MAKE A COPY FOR YOUR FILE.

25. REVIEW JOB INVOICES FOR FINAL APPROVAL OR ADDITIONAL CHANGES.

26. AFTER ALL JOBS ARE COMPLETED, SPEAK WITH THE OWNER TO SEE IF THEY ARE HAPPY AND SIGN OFF THE WORK FOR YOUR FILES. TAKE "AFTER" PHOTOS FOR THE OFFICE & YOUR FILES AND TAKE A LOT! WARRANTY WORK IS FOR ANOTHER DEPARTMENT.

27. CREATE AND SEND WARRANTY INFORMATION TO YOUR OWNER.

28. SEND YOUR OWNER A LINK OR QR CODE TO LEAVE YOU AGREAT ONLINE REVIEW ON YOUR COMPANY WEBSITE OR GOOGLE OR WHEREVER THEY PREFER.ASK THE HOMEOWNER TO INCLUDE YOUR NAME! PRINT IT AND PUT IN YOUR BOOK!

29. AFTER THE JOB HAS BEEN PAID, SUBMIT THE CAP-OUT(A CALCULATION OF YOUR PAY REQUEST) TO THE OFFICE FOR YOUR COMMISSION:

*Author's notes:* Companies usually call this step different names.

30. CALL YOUR OWNER AND ASK THEM TO SEND YOU A RECOMMENDATION EMAIL FOR YOUR OFFICE & FILES:

*Author's notes:* If completed, this is a great document. After working for years, your book will be significant and impressive. Once you receive this great adulation, please forward it to your boss! I have even left this book for a contracting company owner, and within an hour, I was hired without setting up a job interview!

31. CREATE AND SEND WARRANTY INFORMATION TO YOUR OWNER AND CALL THE OFFICE TO SEE WHEN YOU CAN GO BY AND PICK UP YOUR COMMISSION CHECK!

**STRUCTURE YOUR SPREADSHEET** (in Landscape format), SO YOU CAN HAVE 10-60 JOBS IN ONE SEASON ON ONE SPREADSHEET (<u>ONE</u> HORIZON-

TAL LINE PER OWNER) UNDERNEATH THESE # STEPS (# PER COLUMN) . MOVE YOUR OWNERS NAME DOWN THE LINE AS THEIR JOB PROGRESS-ES. ALSO LEAVE ROOM FOR NOTES IF YOU WANT.

WHEN YOUR OWNERS START SIGNINGJOB STARTS TO MOVE, YOU'LL TRULY ONLY THEN APPRECIATE THE STEPS FOR YOUR INSURANCE CLAIM JOBS, AND FOR ALL OF THE EXTRA TIME YOU TRULY ARE SAVING. ! AS EACH HOMEOWNER GOES THROUGH THE STEPS OF JOB COMPLETION, THEN SLIDE THEM TO THE NEXT STEP. ON ONE SPREAD-SHEET, YOU'LL HAVE ALL OF YOUR JOBS IN ONE GLANCE, AS IF IT WAS A PRODUCTION BOARD. THE INSURANCE STEPS WILL KEEP YOU AWARE OF WHAT IS EXPECTED OF YOU FROM THE INSUR-ANCE COMPANY!

GOOD LUCK, BE SAFE, AND MAY YOU BE BLESSED WITH YOUR EFFORTS AND ENTHUSIASM EACH YEAR. MAY YOU ALWAYS HAVE PLENTY OF WORK.

*Unstable Storm System*

*Austin/Killeen, Texas Hailstorm 2016*

*Softball Size Hail Stone*

# MICROBURST

*Microburst*

# FLORIDA EVENING RAIN STORM

# Haag Global

Per Haag Global's website- Exact verbiage, January2025:

"...Since 1924, Haag, a Salas O'Brien Company, is a multi-faceted forensic engineering and consulting company. Haag provides professional services to the legal industry, the insurance industry, corporations, manufacturers, government entities, and individuals. Since 1924, our growth has resulted directly from our long-standing commitment to quality while expanding our technical knowledge and services. Haag has built a reputation for excellence through the efforts of past and present personnel, and we are proud to continue that tradition today.

The information and/or extensive training re:

Forensic Engineering

Forensic Meteorology

Forensic Architecture

Product & Material Testing

Building Consulting

**Certifications, Training, Books & Tools:**

**https://haageducation.com/s/**

and Fire Investigations

...In the roofing and insurance industries, the phrase "Haag Certified" carries much weight. It indicates that you can effectively and efficiently inspect and assess damage. Your report conclusions have a deeper level of credibility: your Certification training could serve as the extra authority you need if you ever find yourself at odds with another's findings. Ultimately, with the damage assessment techniques gained in your Certification course, you can increase your value as an inspector to your employer and to your clients. Being

Certified could be the reason you get called on a job. Other inspectors lack the skills and knowledge you've gained by passing courses developed and taught by practicing forensic engineers."

Here are their Certified Inspector Licenses:

**Residential Roof Inspector Certification**: The Haag Certified Inspector - Residential Roofs program is designed to make you highly proficient with all major types of residential (steep-slope) roofs. You'll learn how hail and wind interact with roofing, inspection safety techniques, roof area calculations, and applicable codes. You'll also gain comprehensive understanding of manufacture, installation, weathering, hail damage, wind damage, maintenance, mechanical damage, and repair costs for each major roofing type — composition, wood shingle/shake, concrete and clay tile, asbestos, fiber cement, and various synthetic, slate, and metal roofing types. Real-world case studies make the information vivid and memorable.

Prequisites: Inspectors should have completed at least 100 sloped roof inspections as the primary roof inspector to qualify for this certification.

**Commercial Roof Inspector Certification:** In the Haag Certified Inspector - Commercial Roofs program, you'll learn to assess damage to all major types of commercial (low-slope and flat) roofing systems. You'll become well versed in inspection safety, roof area calculations, codes and industry standards, and weather characteristics. For each roofing type discussed, instructors profile manufacture, installation, weathering, hail damage, wind damage, maintenance, mechanical damage, and repair costs. The course covers built-up roofing, polymer-modified bitumen roofing, thermoplastic single-ply roofs (PVC and TPO), thermoset plastic single-ply roofs (EPDM, CSPE, PIB), SPF roofing, metal roofing, vegetated (green) roofing, low-slope roofing components, and roof coatings. Case studies illustrate real-world inspection scenarios.

Prerequisites: Inspectors should have completed at least 50 flat roof inspections as the primary roof inspector OR have a minimum of 3 years of commercial lines property adjusting/estimating to qualify for this certification.

**Wind Damage Inspector Certification:** Holding Haag's Wind Damage Certification will show that you have an advanced understanding of wind types and related wind effects, for the purpose of accurately inspecting and assessing an entire building following a wind event. Participants gain an in-depth understanding of all types of wind events (straight-line, tornadic, down-burst, hurricane) and their effects on major types of steep-slope and low-slope roofing systems. They also learn advanced techniques to evaluate and document damage to an entire building envelope (not just the roof) following a wind event. Further, students develop the skills to differentiate wind damage from conditions caused by other factors, both natural and mechanical.

Prerequisites: Inspectors should have completed 50 commercial roof inspections as the primary roof inspector OR have an HCI-R or HCI-C certification to qualify for the HCI-W certification.

*And/or their latest and newest certification:*

**HCI-Master Level Certification:** When you've gained all three HCI certifications, what's next? Haag's most prestigious and highest level of damage assessment certification is now available! The HCI-Master Level is an advanced certification designed for experts in Residential Roofs, Commercial Roofs, and Wind Damage. Acheiving the HCI-Master Level signals an elite understanding and mastery of Haag's industry-leading certifications and damage assessment practices, all founded on Haag's 100-years of scientific hands-on field and laboratory experience. The HCI-Master Level exam will test and affirm an inspector's knowledge of the damage assessment principles found in each certification.

Prerequisites: Once a damage assessment professional has successfully completed each of hte HCI programs individually, they will qualify for the HCI-Master Level certification exam. No additional coursework is required. However, all individual certifications must be active (not expired) to qualify for the HCI-Master Level exam.

***They also have other roof material certifications.***

# Chapter Twenty-One

# Named Storms in the U.S. 2024

As of October 25, 2024, 15 tropical cyclones have formed in the Atlantic hurricane season, and all of them became named storms:

- Hurricanes: 10 storms became hurricanes, including four major hurricanes

- Landfall: 10 systems made landfall The 2024 Atlantic hurricane season began on June 1 and will end on November 30. While not the big season forecasters predicted, the number of named storms is close to the NOAA forecast.

Some notable features of the 2024 Atlantic hurricane season include:

- High hurricane conversion rate: 67% of the season's named storms have become hurricanes, compared to 50% in an average season

- Unusual lull: There hasn't been such a long stretch without hurricane formations between August and September since 1968

- Warm ocean temperatures: Warm to record warm ocean temperatures across much of the Atlantic

- Texas had the most hailstorms in the United States **in 2024**, with more than **500 recorded** events. Other notable hailstorms in 2024 include:

- June 12-14 Damaging hail, high winds, and tornadoes impacted several central and eastern states. Central and northern Minnesota received quarter to golf ball-sized hail, while Omaha, Nebraska experienced up to baseball-sized hail.

- July 31 Giant hail was reported in Stevens

County, the largest reported in at least 38 years.

- Hail is generated when thunderstorms circulate raindrops into the upper layers of the atmosphere.

- The four states that receive the most hail are Kansas, Texas, Oklahoma, and Nebraska.

- The area where Nebraska, Colorado, and Wyoming is known as the Central U.S. "Hail Alley", and averages seven to nine hail days per year.

- Colorado is often considered the hail capital of the U.S., but areas in Wyoming, Montana, South Dakota, Nebraska, and New Mexico may also challenge it.

- Kansas down to San Antonio, on the 1-35 corridor, is also known as "hail alley."

- On June 3, 1959, hail accumulated 18" deep on a levee in Sheldon, Kansas, perhaps the greatest on-level hail accumulation on record in the U.S.

# Chapter Twenty-Two

# Funny Scary Stories

**1.** Secretly, I think the company I started working for wanted to see if I could do the job, so they sent me on my first lead to a straight-up two-story, which means there's nothing for you to set your ladder on that would be at the first story level. Not another roof, not a carport, not an addition for you to climb up and put another ladder on *it* to climb up to the second story. A straight-up two-story means there is nothing like that available. A crew was there on the roof waiting for me. You have to get up there whether it's windy or not, so you want your cougar paws so you don't slip, but inside, I was shaking! I had never been on a tall ladder, which shook the higher I rose. I got through walking up, gripping the ladder and white-knuckled hands. Then I got to the roof part, and four roofers were waiting on me to show me the damage; I had to take pictures of the damage, which meant I had to stand up and walk around. The wind blows harder 20 feet up, so they picked up on my unhappiness. But they never said a word. I got through that, and then the most horrific part was going down. Remember, a home's roof overhang is usually anywhere from 2-4 feet out from the house, meaning I had to go to the roof's edge, swing myself around, and climb down that shaky ladder. I was terrified when I saw what was below me, and only then did I realize that when you get on a roof, you DON'T LOOK DOWN. You can look around and you can look at your feet while you are on the roof, but don't ever look over the edge. Only seasoned roofers and inspectors can stand on the edge of a structure and be okay with their surroundings. All of this was a good thing. It pushed my limits, and I was fine when I was on the ground. I promised myself <u>every day I would do something that scared me</u> because you have to live, and that's life. As long as you're being smart about it and not being irresponsible, it's perfect to challenge your fears. You will be shocked at how strong you truly are.

it's perfect to challenge your fears. You will be shocked at how strong you truly are.

**2.** I was assigned to a large one-story composite. The owner said he had to take his daughter to school and he would be right back. He left me to set up and start doing my inspection. I put the ladder on the front of the house and walked around all the front slopes; I think there were probably five front slopes to review for hail damage. I completed that part of my inspection and then went to the back slopes on the back side of the house. They had a large row of tall Pine trees on the back side of the property and on that side of the subdivision, and his house backed up to the tree line, except maybe there was about an acre between the house and the tree line. The trees were tall, with the sun coming up behind them. It was a beautiful day and early. I did see shaded areas on the back slopes, but I assumed they were shadows from the trees. So, I was on a proper, long hip line at the very top and on both slopes, straddling both, and then I stepped a foot into the shaded area. The shaded area was not shade - it was condensation. It was early morning! A roof's job is to shed water – not absorb it, so it's undeniably there. I had slipped with one leg on one side of the hip and the other leg on the other side of the hip. I dropped everything to try to grip the slopes. I slid down this long hip of thick hip-ridge composite shingles, grabbing anything I could to slow down my momentum. I was flying down. I dug my feet into the roof to ensure that when I came off the house's back corner, the gutters could stop me if installed correctly and IF my toes could catch the gutter's edge. I could drop my feet into them to stop me when I got there. They did! I had wet shingles all around me. By the time I stopped, I was bleeding all over my hands and knees, dripping blood, in a corner of a roof on the house, lying down with my weight on the shingles and shoes inside the corner gutter connection - with no ladder in sight! I had to get myself out of this and off this roof. I was alone. You want to stay very low as you escape a situation like this by laying low while taking one foot/crawl at a time. I also looked at the left side of the roof-hip was in the sunshine, meaning no condensation. I then slowly, very slowly crawled to that side, crawled my way back up to the highest point of the house and got on the front side. I returned to the middle dividing ridge and took my inspection notes of the back slopes with pictures "to finish from afar, lol." If you are an experienced inspector, you can do this with experience and a really good camera. Then I went down to the ladder, and by the time I got down, the owner drove up and got out of the car; he looked and saw the blood on my pants, then all over my hands, with my clothes half wet; he asked what's going on! Are you okay??? Always be fine unless incapacitated! An owner does not want to see an accident on their property, and you're not there to cause him or his property more harm; I explained what happened very calmly. Then I walked around to the back corner with him, and we looked at the corner at the gutter line; the gutter was fine, so he seemed to be a little impressed that I was still happy and walking around like I was when he first met me, but it taught me some great lessons. In this job, you will learn something daily, and <u>NEVER ASSUME IN CONSTRUCTION</u>!

# Chapter Twenty-Three

# CONCLUSION

***I hope you are kind enough*** *to give a retired, fellow independent contractor* a 5-star positive review on Amazon. Your review will be read and greatly appreciated! Only purchasers of this book can leave me a review, so it goes a long way, and frankly, they are tough to get with everything moving so fast these days. The easiest way to do this is to aim your smartphone camera at the QR Code below, and when your screen notifies you of a website, tap on the yellow alert - with your finger, and you'll be taken there so easily....

*QR CODE FOR EASY ACCESS TO LEAVE REVIEW : )*

You are greatly appreciated! This book will enhance your career, and I am glad you enjoyed my first book! Remember you are not alone in this industry.

-D Cummins

# Chapter Twenty-Four

# References

TDI TexasDept. of Insurance:https://www.tdi.texas.gov/agent/adjuster-all-lines-apply.html

GoogleMaps.com: https://www.google.com/maps

HaagEngineering: https://haagglobal.com/

FEMA:https://www.fema.gov/faq/employment-home-inspector-fema

Wikipedia.com

Reddit.com

YouTube.com

Xactimate Estimate Training: https://www.verisk.com/products/xactimate/training/

It AlwaysWill Be – Song by WillieNelson: https://www.youtube.com/watch?v=dzl7yc-GEoBE

The GoatLadder System: https://thegoatsteepassist.com/

Weather& Radar: https://www.youtube.com/@weatherandradarUSA